Published by Ice House Books
Copyright © 2019 Ice House Books

Illustrations by Janet Samuel

Ice House Books is an imprint of Half Moon Bay Limited
The Ice House, 124 Walcot Street, Bath, BA1 5BG
www.icehousebooks.co.uk

ISBN 978-1-912867-58-5

Printed in China

While **Shepherds** Watched

While shepherds watched their flocks by night ...

... all seated on the ground.

The angel of the
Lord came down ...

... and glory shone around.

"Fear not," said he for mighty dread ...

... had seized their
troubled mind.

"Glad tidings of
great joy I bring ...

"... to you and all mankind."

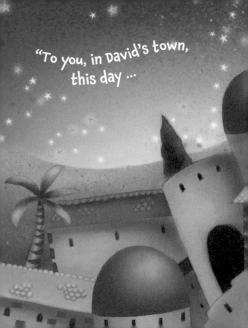

"To you, in David's town,
this day ...

... is born of David's line,"

"A Saviour, who is Christ the Lord ...

"... and this shall be the sign."

"The heavenly Babe
    you there shall find ..."

"... to human view displayed."

"All meanly wrapped
in swathing bands ...

"... and in a manger laid."

Thus spake the seraph,
and forthwith ...

... appeared a shining throng ...

... of angels praising God
who thus,

... addressed their joyful song.

"All glory be to God on high ...

... and on Earth be peace."

"Good will henceforth
from heaven to me ...

... begin and never cease."

The End